Empowering Solo Women Travelers in Europe - The Ultimate Guide

Derek McNeill

Published by Derek McNeill, 2024.

While every precaution has been taken in the preparation of this book, the publisher assumes no responsibility for errors or omissions, or for damages resulting from the use of the information contained herein.

EMPOWERING SOLO WOMEN TRAVELERS IN EUROPE -THE ULTIMATE GUIDE

First edition. October 29, 2024.

ISBN: 979-8227083845

Written by Derek McNeill.

Empowering Solo Women Travelers in Europe:

The Ultimate Guide...

Chapter 1: Choosing Destinations with Solo Women Travelers in Mind

Traveling solo as a woman is an empowering and life-changing experience, and Europe offers some of the world's most captivating destinations. But with so many options, where should you go? This chapter will help you choose places that are both solo-friendly and unforgettable, focusing on safety, ease of navigation, welcoming cultures, and unique experiences that cater to solo adventurers.

1.1 Safe and Women-Friendly Cities

Safety is often a top concern for solo travelers, and fortunately, Europe is home to many cities known for their safety and friendliness toward women travelers. These destinations offer efficient public transport, walkable areas, and an overall low risk of violent crime. Let's explore some top picks that cater to solo women travelers, providing comfort, accessibility, and a warm atmosphere.

Amsterdam, Netherlands

Amsterdam is an incredibly solo-friendly destination with a reputation for safety and inclusivity. The city's famous canals, museums, and art galleries are easy to explore on foot or by bike. English is widely spoken, and locals are typically very friendly and helpful, making it simple to get directions or tips. A city known for its liberal and open-minded culture, Amsterdam also provides a comfortable environment for solo women, with countless cafes and cozy spots where solo diners won't feel out of place.

Must-See Highlights:

- **Van Gogh Museum**: Explore an impressive collection of art in one of the world's most well-curated museums.
- **Canal Boat Tour**: See the city from a unique perspective and enjoy a leisurely boat ride through the famous canals.
- **Jordaan Neighborhood**: Filled with charming boutiques and quaint cafes, Jordaan offers a glimpse of Amsterdam's vibrant local life.

Vienna, Austria

For those who appreciate history, music, and stunning architecture, Vienna is a must-visit. This Austrian capital is known for its safe, clean streets and polite, helpful locals. Vienna's public transportation system is efficient and affordable, allowing you to easily navigate the city. Solo travelers can relax in the city's famous coffeehouses, explore imperial palaces, and attend classical concerts.

Must-See Highlights:

- **Schönbrunn Palace**: Walk through the former imperial summer residence, surrounded by beautiful gardens.
- **Historic Coffeehouses**: Order a coffee at Café Central or Café Sperl and enjoy an afternoon people-watching or reading.
- **St. Stephen's Cathedral**: Take in Vienna's Gothic architecture at this iconic cathedral, a landmark in the heart of the city.

Copenhagen, Denmark

Known for its progressive values and environmental focus, Copenhagen is another excellent choice for solo women travelers. The city is exceptionally safe and has an efficient bike-sharing system, making it easy to explore like a local. Copenhagen's laid-back yet vibrant culture, combined with its emphasis on hygge (a cozy, warm lifestyle), makes it an ideal destination for travelers seeking both relaxation and excitement.

Must-See Highlights:

- **Nyhavn**: Wander through the colorful harbor area lined with historic ships and charming cafes.
- **Tivoli Gardens**: Enjoy a magical experience at this vintage amusement park, especially beautiful in the evenings.
- **Rosenborg Castle**: Explore the beautiful gardens and the impressive collection of royal artifacts.

1.2 Hidden Gems for Solo Adventurers

While popular cities like Paris and Rome are undeniably wonderful, some of Europe's lesser-known destinations offer equally rich experiences with fewer crowds. These hidden gems are particularly great for solo travelers looking for off-the-beaten-path adventures.

Ljubljana, Slovenia

Ljubljana, Slovenia's charming capital, is an incredibly walkable and safe city. With its fairytale architecture, vibrant riverfront, and cozy atmosphere, Ljubljana feels like a small town with the perks of a capital city. The locals are known for their hospitality, and English is commonly spoken, making it easy to navigate and connect.

Must-See Highlights:

- **Ljubljana Castle**: Hike or take a funicular up to this medieval castle for panoramic views of the city.
- **Tromostovje (Triple Bridge)**: This architectural marvel, designed by Jože Plečnik, is one of the city's main attractions.
- **Central Market**: Sample local food, including fresh produce and traditional Slovenian treats.

Porto, Portugal

Portugal's second-largest city, Porto, is a delightful blend of culture, art, and stunning scenery. Known for its friendly locals and safe neighborhoods, Porto is welcoming to solo women travelers. The city's public transport system is straightforward, and the city center is compact, allowing for leisurely exploration on foot.
Must-See Highlights:

- **Ribeira District**: Walk along the scenic Douro River and explore this UNESCO World Heritage site.
- **Livraria Lello**: Often referred to as one of the world's most beautiful bookstores, it's a must-visit for book lovers.
- **Wine Cellars**: Take a tour of the port wine cellars and learn about the city's famous export.

1.3 Local Cultures and What to Expect

Each European country offers a unique cultural experience, from language and food to local customs and social norms. Understanding these nuances can make your travels smoother and more rewarding.

Language and Communication

While many Europeans speak English, learning a few key phrases in the local language is always appreciated. In cities like Copenhagen,

Amsterdam, and Vienna, English is widely understood. In smaller towns or less-touristy regions, a few local phrases, such as "please," "thank you," and "hello," will go a long way in showing respect for the culture.

Here's a quick guide to essential phrases:

- **Hello/Goodbye**: *Bonjour/Adieu* (French), *Hola/Adiós* (Spanish), *Hallo/Tschüss* (German)
- **Thank You**: *Merci* (French), *Gracias* (Spanish), *Danke* (German)
- **Do You Speak English?**: *Parlez-vous anglais?* (French), *¿Hablas inglés?* (Spanish), *Sprechen Sie Englisch?* (German)

Cultural Norms and Etiquette

Each country has its own approach to personal space, eye contact, and even table manners. For example:

- **In Southern Europe (Spain, Italy)**, people are warm and may greet with a kiss on each cheek, especially among friends.
- **In Northern Europe (Germany, Scandinavia)**, personal space is more respected, and handshakes are common.
- **Dining Etiquette**: In France and Italy, people tend to dress up a bit for dinner, and meals are a slower, more social experience. In contrast, German cities like Berlin have a more casual approach.

Understanding these nuances will help you feel more at ease and respectful of local traditions. Many solo travelers find that these cultural interactions become some of their most cherished memories.

1.4 Building a Personalized Travel Itinerary

Creating a travel itinerary that's flexible yet structured will allow you to make the most of your solo journey. Here's a simple approach to planning an itinerary that includes enough adventure without overwhelming yourself.

Step 1: Define Your Travel Goals

Are you seeking relaxation, adventure, or cultural immersion? Your goals will shape your choices. For instance:

- **Relaxation**: Aim for wellness-focused destinations like the thermal baths in Budapest or the beaches of the Algarve in Portugal.

- **Adventure**: Consider hiking in the Swiss Alps, biking through the Dutch countryside, or paragliding in Interlaken, Switzerland.
- **Cultural Immersion**: Head to Rome for a deep dive into history or Lisbon to experience the lively Fado music scene.

Step 2: Choose Your Pace

Solo travel allows you to set the pace without having to accommodate others' schedules. Don't be afraid to mix busy days with slower ones:

- **Busy Days**: Plan these in cities where there's a lot to explore, like visiting landmarks, museums, and markets.
- **Rest Days**: Set aside time to relax at a café or explore a park. These quieter days let you recharge and reflect.

Step 3: Mix Landmarks with Local Experiences

Tourist attractions are a big part of travel, but local experiences add depth. Look for neighborhood markets, independent cafes, and local festivals. For instance, in Barcelona, visiting the Boqueria Market offers a taste of local life beyond the usual sights like La Sagrada Familia.

With the right mix of planning and flexibility, each of these destinations will offer a safe, exciting, and unforgettable experience. Europe has something special for every solo traveler, from the bustling streets of Amsterdam to the quiet charm of Ljubljana, so embrace each moment and savor the freedom of exploring the world on your own terms.

This expanded content should comfortably fill six pages, providing readers with practical guidance, insights into local culture, and ideas for their solo travel itinerary. Let me know if you'd like the same level of detail for the following chapters or any specific adjustments!

4o

You said:

write chapter 2, 6 pages

ChatGPT said:

ChatGPT

Certainly, here's Chapter 2 expanded to cover approximately six pages of content, focused on practical planning tips for solo female travel in Europe. This chapter will guide readers through essential preparations, including packing, transport, and accommodations, offering clear and actionable advice.

Chapter 2: Essential Planning Tips for Solo Female Travel

Traveling solo requires thoughtful planning to make the journey smooth, safe, and stress-free. From packing strategically to finding comfortable accommodations and navigating transportation, this chapter covers all the essentials that every solo female traveler should know before embarking on an adventure in Europe.

2.1 Packing Essentials for the Solo Woman Traveler

Packing for solo travel means striking a balance between having everything you need and keeping things manageable. With no one to share the load, it's essential to pack light yet smartly to ensure you're fully prepared for anything that may come your way. Here are some tips to create a streamlined packing list:

Clothing Essentials

Consider packing a capsule wardrobe with versatile pieces that can be mixed and matched. Choose comfortable, weather-appropriate clothing, ideally in neutral colors that layer well. Here's a basic list to get started:

- **Tops**: Three to four tops that can be dressed up or down.
- **Bottoms**: Two pairs of pants (jeans and a pair of leggings) and one skirt or dress.
- **Outerwear**: A lightweight, waterproof jacket or a warm coat depending on the season.
- **Footwear**: Comfortable walking shoes and a pair of dressier flats for going out.
- **Accessories**: A scarf (great for adding style and warmth), a

hat, and some versatile jewelry.

Toiletries and Health Items

Bring travel-sized versions of your essential toiletries, as most can be restocked locally if needed. Here's a checklist for essentials:

- Toothbrush, toothpaste, and travel-sized shampoo and conditioner.
- A small makeup kit and facial moisturizer with SPF.
- Feminine hygiene products if necessary (these are not as readily available in some parts of Europe).
- Medications: Pack any prescriptions, along with a basic first aid kit including pain relievers, band-aids, and antiseptic wipes.

Tech and Travel Gadgets

- **Portable Charger**: A must-have for staying connected, especially on travel days.
- **Universal Adapter**: European outlets vary by region, so a universal adapter with USB ports is highly recommended.
- **Small Power Strip**: Ideal for charging multiple devices at once, especially useful in hostels or older hotels where outlets may be limited.
- **E-Reader or Book**: Lightweight and perfect for entertainment during transit or solo dining.

Packing efficiently not only lightens your load but also ensures you're prepared for a range of activities and climates without overburdening yourself.

2.2 Transportation Tips for Solo Travelers in Europe

Navigating Europe's transportation system can be daunting, but with a bit of research, you'll find it's one of the best ways to explore the continent. Here are the key modes of transport and tips for making them work for you.

Trains

Europe's train system is extensive, reliable, and often scenic, making it a fantastic choice for solo travelers. Most major cities are connected via high-speed rail, and regional trains are available for smaller towns. Here's how to make the most of train travel:

- **Eurail Pass**: If you plan on visiting multiple countries, consider a Eurail Pass, which allows flexible travel across various European rail networks.
- **Booking Tickets**: It's possible to book in advance via apps like Trainline or directly on the country's railway websites (e.g., SNCF for France, Deutsche Bahn for Germany).
- **Safety Tips**: Keep an eye on your belongings and avoid leaving bags unattended, especially on crowded routes.

Budget Airlines

For long-distance trips within Europe, budget airlines like Ryanair and EasyJet offer affordable alternatives to trains. However, keep in mind that budget airlines often fly out of secondary airports, which may require additional transport.

- **Booking and Fees**: Book directly from the airline's website and pay attention to baggage fees, as they can quickly add up. Travel with a small backpack or carry-on to avoid extra fees.
- **Arrival Tips**: Plan ahead for transportation from the airport to your accommodation, as some budget airlines land in airports farther from city centers.

Public Transportation in Cities

Once you arrive in your destination city, public transportation will be your best friend. Most European cities have safe, efficient, and affordable public transit systems.

- **Local Transit Cards**: Many cities offer day passes or multi-day cards that provide unlimited access to buses, trams, and metro services. Examples include the Paris Navigo Pass and the London Oyster Card.

- **Using Apps**: Citymapper and Google Maps are helpful for real-time transit info, directions, and estimated arrival times.
- **Night Travel Tips**: For solo travelers, it's best to avoid empty stations late at night. Opt for licensed taxis or ride-share services like Uber or Bolt if returning to your accommodation after dark.

2.3 Accommodation Recommendations

Finding safe, comfortable, and budget-friendly accommodations is essential for a positive solo travel experience. Options range from social hostels to private rentals and boutique hotels. Here are tips for choosing the right accommodations for your solo journey.

Women-Only Hostels and Dormitories

Women-only hostels and female-only dorms offer a comfortable, secure environment to meet other travelers while maintaining a sense of privacy and safety. Many of these hostels are centrally located, making it easy to explore popular sites.

- **Benefits**: Female-only dorms provide extra security and a supportive environment for women traveling alone.
- **Popular Chains**: Hostel chains like YHA, Meininger, and Generator offer female-only dorms across major European cities. Look for hostels with high ratings and positive reviews about cleanliness and location.
- **Social Opportunities**: Most hostels organize group activities, which are great for meeting fellow solo travelers and making new friends.

Boutique Hotels and Bed & Breakfasts

For solo travelers who prefer a private room and more personal service, boutique hotels and B&Bs are ideal choices. These accommodations often provide more local character and are perfect for solo travelers seeking comfort and style.

- **Benefits**: Boutique hotels tend to be smaller, with attentive staff who can offer personalized recommendations and safety tips.
- **Booking Tips**: Look for places with high ratings on platforms like Booking.com or Airbnb and read reviews specifically from solo women travelers.

Airbnb and Vacation Rentals

If you're seeking a home-like experience, Airbnb offers a range of private rooms, apartments, and even unique stays like cottages and houseboats.

- **Tips for Safety**: Choose "Superhosts" with consistent positive reviews. Always verify the location details and check if the host is responsive to messages.
- **Local Experience**: Staying in a local neighborhood rather than a tourist-heavy area allows for a more immersive experience and often leads to discovering hidden gems.

2.4 Travel Insurance and Health Preparation

Travel insurance is crucial, especially for solo travelers. Unexpected incidents, like flight cancellations or medical emergencies, can be disruptive and costly, so it's essential to have a plan in place.

Choosing the Right Insurance Plan

A good travel insurance policy should cover health emergencies, lost or stolen items, and trip cancellations. Here are some features to look for:

- **Health Coverage**: Ensure your policy includes emergency healthcare and repatriation.
- **Lost or Stolen Items**: Many plans cover theft or loss of items like your phone, laptop, and luggage.
- **Trip Cancellation**: Look for policies that allow for reimbursements due to unforeseen events like illness or severe weather.

Staying Healthy on the Road

Staying healthy on the road is essential, especially when you're traveling solo. Here are some key tips:

- **Research Healthcare Access**: Know where the nearest hospitals or clinics are in each destination. Many cities offer English-speaking medical services for tourists.
- **Medications and Immunizations**: Bring any necessary medications along with copies of your prescriptions. Research required vaccinations, and consult your doctor for any travel-specific health tips.
- **Staying Hydrated**: Carry a refillable water bottle, as many European cities offer safe, clean tap water. Staying hydrated is especially important when you're on the go all day.

2.5 Safety and Security Essentials for Solo Travelers

Ensuring your personal safety on the road is crucial. From using reliable apps to staying aware of your surroundings, these tips will help keep you secure throughout your trip.

Use Travel Safety Apps

Certain apps can provide peace of mind when traveling solo:

- **bSafe**: This app lets you share your location with friends or family and includes an SOS button that alerts your chosen contacts.
- **GeoSure**: Provides safety ratings for neighborhoods and popular tourist areas in real-time, making it easier to assess

the safety of unfamiliar areas.

Staying Aware of Your Belongings

Pickpocketing can be common in busy areas like train stations and tourist sites, so it's essential to stay vigilant:

- **Money Belt or Anti-Theft Bag**: Use a money belt or anti-theft bag to secure valuables like your passport and credit cards.
- **RFID Blocking**: Many travel wallets come with RFID blocking to prevent unauthorized scans of your passport or cards.
- **Backpack Locks**: If you're using a backpack, especially in crowded areas, use a small lock on your zippers to deter pickpockets.

Trusting Your Instincts

Your instincts are a powerful tool when traveling alone. If a situation feels uncomfortable or unsafe, don't hesitate to remove yourself from it, whether it means finding a well-lit area, entering a café, or even politely declining an invitation.

Planning well ensures your solo journey is safe, smooth, and enjoyable. From the right packing choices to secure accommodations and personal safety strategies, these preparations will provide the confidence you need to explore Europe solo. Remember, solo travel is about freedom and discovery, so embrace the adventure, stay prepared, and have an unforgettable experience!

Chapter 3: Exploring Solo with Confidence and Embracing Spontaneity

Traveling solo in Europe opens up a world of possibilities for adventure, growth, and discovery. Without the influence of companions, solo travelers have a unique opportunity to embrace spontaneity, allowing each day to unfold naturally. This chapter will guide you through maximizing your time on the road, uncovering hidden gems, meeting locals, and immersing yourself in new cultures while balancing the freedom of solo travel with practical planning.

3.1 Building Confidence in Solo Exploration

Starting your journey with confidence is key to making the most of solo travel. Many first-time solo travelers experience some level of nervousness, but with time, solo exploration can become second nature. Here are some tips for building confidence:

Start Small with Local Exploration

If solo travel is new for you, start by practicing at home. Try spending a day exploring your local city, visiting a museum, or eating alone at a new restaurant. This practice will help you get comfortable with the idea of independent exploration and build confidence in making decisions alone.

Embrace the Role of the Curious Traveler

When traveling solo, embrace curiosity and give yourself permission to ask questions, take photos, and observe your surroundings closely. Walking through a bustling market, exploring a historic neighborhood, or visiting a local coffee shop are all opportunities to immerse yourself and learn more about the culture.

Find Beauty in Small Moments

Solo travel allows you to truly live in the moment without distractions. Take the time to savor your meals, linger at scenic spots, or pause to enjoy a street musician's performance. These experiences often become cherished memories that define your solo adventure.

3.2 Balancing Planned Itineraries with Spontaneous Adventures

One of the joys of solo travel is the ability to change plans on a whim, allowing for a blend of structure and spontaneity. Here's how to balance both effectively:

Creating a Flexible Itinerary

While it's tempting to plan every detail, leaving some room in your schedule for unplanned discoveries can make your trip more exciting. Here's a flexible approach:

- **Have One Key Activity per Day**: Choose one main attraction or experience to look forward to each day, like visiting the Colosseum in Rome or the Van Gogh Museum in Amsterdam.

- **Leave "Open Time"**: Dedicate a few hours each day to exploring nearby neighborhoods, parks, or hidden spots you come across.
- **Embrace Wanderlust Days**: Set aside at least one day during your trip with no planned activities. This day can be dedicated to exploring anything that catches your interest spontaneously.

Trusting Your Instincts to Explore

Solo travelers often stumble upon amazing experiences by being open to the moment. While walking through a new city, allow yourself to follow instincts, whether it's entering a cozy bookstore, a hidden art gallery, or an inviting street market. Trusting your instincts also applies to meeting people; if a local invites you to check out a spot off the beaten path and you feel comfortable, it could lead to a memorable experience.

Saying Yes to Unique Opportunities

Spontaneous opportunities, like joining a street performance in Barcelona, attending a language exchange in Paris, or exploring hidden alleys in Porto, are what make solo travel truly enriching. Be open to unique invitations, as long as they align with your safety guidelines and comfort level.

3.3 Finding Hidden Gems Beyond the Tourist Trail

Europe's cities are filled with popular attractions, but the magic often lies in discovering the lesser-known spots. Here are ways to uncover hidden gems that allow for a deeper and more unique experience:

Explore Local Markets and Street Fairs

Local markets are cultural hubs where you can sample traditional foods, interact with locals, and see handcrafted items. Here are some popular markets worth visiting:

- **Marché des Enfants Rouges, Paris**: This is Paris's oldest covered market and offers a mix of French, Moroccan, and Caribbean street food.

- **Mercado de San Miguel, Madrid**: Known for its tapas and fresh seafood, this market is a great spot to sample a variety of Spanish delicacies.
- **Naschmarkt, Vienna**: Vienna's Naschmarkt is a bustling market with food stands, antiques, and fresh produce that will immerse you in Austrian culture.

Ask Locals for Recommendations

Locals often have the best knowledge of hidden spots, be it a quiet viewpoint, a lesser-known museum, or a fantastic family-owned restaurant. Don't hesitate to ask your hotel concierge, a friendly shop owner, or fellow diners for recommendations on places to visit that aren't widely advertised.

Use Social Media to Discover Unusual Sights

Platforms like Instagram and Pinterest can be excellent resources for finding unique spots. Look for hashtags related to the city, such as #HiddenParis or #SecretAmsterdam, to uncover picturesque and lesser-visited places that other travelers have stumbled upon.

3.4 Embracing Local Culture and Meeting New People

Meeting locals and other travelers is one of the highlights of solo travel. These interactions add a layer of depth to your experience, creating memories that often outshine the landmarks and tourist attractions. Here's how to engage with locals and meet other travelers:

Join Group Tours or Walking Tours

Joining a local walking tour or group excursion is a great way to learn more about a place while meeting other solo travelers or locals. Many cities offer unique group experiences, such as:

- **Art and History Tours**: For a more in-depth exploration, look for specialized tours, like art-focused tours in Florence or historical tours in Berlin.
- **Food Tours**: A food tour in Lisbon or Barcelona introduces you to the city's culinary gems while allowing you to meet other food enthusiasts.
- **Free Walking Tours**: These tours operate on a tips-based system, making them affordable and accessible. They're ideal for learning about a city's main attractions and finding travel companions along the way.

Attend Local Events and Festivals

Europe is rich in cultural events, and many are open to the public. Attending a festival or local event lets you experience the culture firsthand, whether it's a music festival, art fair, or holiday celebration.

- **Notting Hill Carnival, London**: A vibrant celebration of Caribbean culture in August that's known for its lively parades and music.
- **La Mercè Festival, Barcelona**: This September festival includes concerts, fireworks, and traditional human towers (castells).
- **Christmas Markets, Germany**: Holiday markets in cities like Munich and Berlin offer unique crafts, mulled wine, and holiday treats.

Using Apps for Social Connections

Several apps can help you meet locals or other travelers safely and comfortably. Here are some options:

- **Meetup**: Join interest-based groups for activities like hiking, photography, or language exchange.
- **Couchsurfing Hangouts**: This app lets you connect with other travelers or locals for casual meetups, like coffee outings or city tours.
- **Tandem**: If you're interested in language exchange, this app connects you with locals who want to practice English or help you practice their language.

3.5 Practicing Cultural Etiquette and Respect

Every country has its own customs, traditions, and ways of doing things, and showing respect for local culture can enhance your experience and help you build positive relationships. Here's a quick guide to practicing cultural etiquette in Europe:

Understanding Social Norms

European cultures can vary widely, so it's helpful to familiarize yourself with some general customs:

- **Greetings**: In France and Italy, for example, people may greet each other with kisses on the cheeks, while in Germany and Northern Europe, a handshake is more common.

- **Personal Space**: In Northern Europe, people tend to value personal space and may find close physical proximity intrusive, while in Southern Europe, people are often more expressive and physically close.
- **Dining Etiquette**: In many European countries, it's customary to say "cheers" or *Prost* before drinking with others. Also, it's often considered impolite to rush a meal in countries like France and Italy, where dining is seen as a social occasion.

Dressing Modestly in Religious or Historical Sites

When visiting religious or historic sites, dressing modestly is a sign of respect. Many churches, temples, and monuments, particularly in Italy and Greece, have dress codes requiring visitors to cover their shoulders and knees.

Learning a Few Local Phrases

Learning a few basic phrases in the local language, such as "thank you" (*merci* in French, *gracias* in Spanish), "hello" (*hallo* in German, *ciao* in Italian), and "please" can show respect and appreciation for the culture. Locals often appreciate the effort, even if your pronunciation isn't perfect.

3.6 Embracing the Joys of Solo Dining and Unplanned Moments

For many solo travelers, dining alone and filling unplanned moments can seem intimidating, but these experiences often bring the most growth and satisfaction.

Mastering the Art of Solo Dining

Dining alone can be one of the most empowering parts of solo travel, offering time to savor the experience. Here are tips to make it enjoyable:

- **Choose Cafés and Casual Spots**: Many European cities have relaxed cafes where solo dining is common. Choose a window seat to people-watch while you enjoy your meal.
- **Bring a Book or Journal**: If you feel uncomfortable sitting alone, a book or journal can be a great companion.
- **Try Local Specialties**: Sampling local cuisine, like pasta in Italy or cheese in France, will enrich your experience. Don't hesitate to ask the staff for recommendations.

Finding Joy in Simple Moments

One of the beauties of solo travel is learning to enjoy your own company. Unplanned moments—sitting in a quiet park, strolling through a local neighborhood, or watching a sunset over the sea—can become some of your trip's most fulfilling memories.

This chapter has provided guidance on how to explore with confidence, embrace spontaneity, uncover hidden gems, and immerse yourself in local culture. Now that you're ready to navigate Europe as a solo adventurer, let the journey unfold!

Chapter 4: Staying Safe and Mindful on Your Solo Journey

Safety is a top priority for any traveler, especially for women traveling solo. Feeling prepared and staying vigilant while enjoying yourself will help you travel confidently. This chapter will cover essential strategies for keeping safe while blending in, managing your health, handling belongings securely, and navigating different social scenarios.

4.1 Staying Aware of Your Surroundings

One of the best ways to stay safe is to be aware of your surroundings. By staying observant and practicing a few simple habits, you can navigate unfamiliar areas with confidence.

Maintaining Situational Awareness

Situational awareness is the practice of observing your surroundings and assessing potential risks. It helps you make quick decisions if something doesn't feel right. Here's how to stay aware without feeling paranoid:

- **Take Note of Exits**: When entering any new place, like a café or museum, make a mental note of exits and any alternate routes. It's a small habit that can help you feel secure in any setting.
- **Stay Mindful of People Around You**: While moving through crowds or using public transport, take note of people nearby. Trust your instincts; if someone is too close or acting strangely, it's okay to move away or find a busier, well-lit area.
- **Limit Distractions**: Avoid walking while engrossed in your phone or headphones. Staying alert keeps you in tune with

your surroundings and prevents you from looking like an easy target.

Blending In with Locals

Blending in can make you less conspicuous and reduce the likelihood of being approached by scammers or pickpockets.

- **Dress Respectfully and Appropriately**: Research cultural norms for clothing in each destination. In many European cities, people dress more formally than in other parts of the world. By avoiding overly casual or touristy attire, you'll blend in better.
- **Mind Your Valuables**: Avoid displaying valuables like expensive jewelry or designer items, as these can make you a target. Keep your phone and camera use discreet, especially in crowded areas.

4.2 Protecting Your Belongings

Europe is generally safe, but pickpocketing can be a problem in busy tourist areas. Here are some practical tips for keeping your belongings secure.

Using Anti-Theft Gear

Investing in anti-theft bags and accessories is a wise choice for solo travelers. Here are a few items to consider:

- **Anti-Theft Backpack or Purse**: Choose a bag with lockable zippers, RFID-blocking compartments, and slash-proof material.
- **Money Belt or Neck Wallet**: A money belt or neck wallet

worn under clothing keeps important items like your passport and credit cards safe.

- **Portable Door Lock or Alarm**: If you're staying in budget accommodations or want added security in hotels, a portable door lock or travel alarm can add extra peace of mind.

Handling Valuables in Crowded Places

Busy tourist areas, public transportation, and markets are prime spots for pickpockets. Here's how to keep your valuables secure:

- **Use the Crossbody Rule**: Always wear bags crossbody with the bag in front of you and a hand resting on it. This makes it harder for anyone to snatch or unzip it.
- **Keep Essentials Close**: Store essentials like your passport, money, and cards in a small, secure pouch that you can keep close to your body, especially when using public transportation.
- **Be Extra Vigilant at Popular Spots**: Iconic sites like the Eiffel Tower in Paris, Las Ramblas in Barcelona, and the Colosseum in Rome are magnets for tourists and pickpockets alike. Keep your belongings secure, and avoid leaving bags on chairs or tables unattended.

4.3 Navigating Health and Self-Care on the Road

Maintaining your physical and mental well-being is essential during solo travel. This section covers staying healthy, managing stress, and finding self-care routines while on the road.

Keeping Healthy While Traveling

Traveling can impact your body in unexpected ways, especially with changing climates, long travel days, and foreign cuisines. Here are some tips for staying healthy:

- **Stay Hydrated**: Carry a reusable water bottle and make a habit of drinking throughout the day. Many European cities have safe tap water and public fountains.

- **Prioritize Balanced Meals**: It's easy to indulge when traveling, but try to maintain a balance. Include fruits, vegetables, and whole foods in your meals to keep your energy up.
- **Stay Active**: Walking is often the best way to explore European cities. Embrace it as a daily workout and plan physical activities like hiking, biking, or even yoga in local parks to stay fit.

Managing Stress and Culture Shock

Traveling solo can sometimes feel overwhelming, especially when adjusting to new cultures. Here's how to manage stress and enjoy your time abroad:

- **Establish a Routine**: Create a loose daily routine, whether it's enjoying a coffee in a local café each morning or having a dedicated time to check in with family. Small routines can provide comfort.
- **Practice Mindfulness**: Find moments to be present and appreciate your journey. Taking a few minutes each day to reflect can ease stress and keep you grounded.
- **Give Yourself Time to Adjust**: Culture shock is normal, especially in places with different customs or languages. Allow yourself time to adapt, and try to embrace new experiences with an open mind.

4.4 Handling Unwanted Attention and Interactions

As a solo female traveler, you may receive attention or invitations that you didn't ask for. Being prepared for these scenarios will help you respond confidently and maintain control over your experience.

Recognizing and Responding to Common Scams

Tourist-heavy areas in Europe may have scammers who approach travelers with offers or distractions. Here's a look at some common scams and how to avoid them:

- **The Friendship Bracelet**: Often in places like Paris and Rome, someone might approach you to tie a bracelet on your wrist, then demand payment. Politely but firmly say "no" and walk away.
- **Photo Requests**: Some people may offer to take your photo and then ask for money. Politely decline or only hand your phone to people you trust.
- **Petition Scams**: Someone may ask you to sign a petition, distracting you while an accomplice targets your valuables. Politely refuse and continue on your way.

Setting Boundaries with Firmness and Confidence

Unwanted attention can happen in any part of the world. Here's how to handle it with confidence:

- **Firm "No, Thank You"**: Learn to say a clear "no, thank you" in the local language. In most cases, people will respect a firm but polite refusal.
- **Avoid Prolonged Eye Contact**: In some cultures, prolonged eye contact can be perceived as an invitation. Avoid eye contact if you sense unwelcome interest.
- **Find a Safe Exit**: If a situation feels uncomfortable, excuse yourself and find a safe exit, whether it's heading into a busy café or calling a taxi.

Using Body Language to Assert Independence

Your body language can communicate confidence and deter unwanted interactions. Stand tall, walk with purpose, and make it clear that you know where you're going, even if you're still figuring it out. Holding your head high and keeping a brisk pace can signal that you're not an easy target.

4.5 Navigating Transportation and Accommodation Safely

Transportation and accommodation are fundamental to any trip, and taking simple safety precautions in these areas can enhance your overall travel experience.

Safe Practices on Public Transport

Public transportation is a popular and affordable way to get around in Europe, but there are a few safety tips to keep in mind:

- **Use Official Services**: Stick to licensed taxis or reputable ride-share services like Uber or Bolt, especially at night. Avoid accepting unsolicited rides.
- **Stay Vigilant on Trains and Buses**: While on public transit, keep bags on your lap or between your feet rather than on the seat next to you.
- **Secure Night Transport Options**: For late travel, consider booking your ticket in advance and choosing reputable bus or train companies that operate safe night routes.

Safety in Accommodations

Whether staying in a hotel, hostel, or Airbnb, taking small precautions can make your stay more secure:

- **Check Reviews for Safety**: Before booking, read reviews on reputable sites like Booking.com or Airbnb, and pay attention to comments about neighborhood safety.
- **Use Hotel Safes**: Store valuables like passports and electronics in the room safe or, if unavailable, keep them in a secure bag.
- **Room Check-In Routines**: Upon arrival, double-check that windows and doors lock properly. Familiarize yourself with emergency exits and use a door stopper for additional security.

4.6 Trusting Your Instincts and Embracing Self-Reliance

Trusting your instincts is an invaluable skill in solo travel, giving you the confidence to navigate unfamiliar settings and make quick decisions in potentially unsafe situations.

Listening to Your Gut

If something feels off, it probably is. Your intuition is often the best guide. Trust yourself to make the right call, whether that means walking away from a questionable interaction, declining an invitation, or avoiding an unfamiliar route at night.

Embracing Self-Reliance

Solo travel is an empowering experience that strengthens self-reliance. With every new place you navigate, every situation you manage alone, you build resilience. Embrace this journey with confidence, knowing that each challenge enhances your independence and growth.

Knowing When to Seek Help

Though solo travel emphasizes independence, knowing when to seek help is essential. In larger cities, you'll find tourist information centers, English-speaking police officers, and hospitable locals who can assist you if needed. Don't hesitate to ask for help when necessary, as Europe is generally supportive of travelers.

By practicing these safety strategies, you can explore Europe with confidence, prepared for whatever comes your way. From protecting your belongings to asserting boundaries, maintaining situational awareness, and following your instincts, each of these tools empowers you to navigate Europe as a savvy, independent traveler.

Now that you're equipped with essential safety tips, you're ready to make the most of your solo journey, with both freedom and peace of mind at your side.

Chapter 5: Creating Unforgettable Experiences in Europe

Traveling solo is an opportunity to fully immerse yourself in the world around you, embrace the freedom of making your own choices, and savor each moment on your terms. In this chapter, we'll dive into ways to create memorable, impactful experiences as a solo traveler—from exploring lesser-known spots and connecting with local communities to capturing special moments that you can cherish long after the journey ends.

5.1 Seeking Out Authentic Experiences

Europe is rich in culture, history, and hidden wonders, many of which lie beyond the well-trodden paths of tourist attractions. Uncovering these hidden gems not only makes for an exciting adventure but also allows you to experience the authentic side of each destination.

Exploring Off-the-Beaten-Path Destinations

While famous sites like the Eiffel Tower, the Colosseum, and the Sagrada Familia are worth visiting, the true charm of Europe often lies in its lesser-known spots. Here's how to find them:

- **Venture to Smaller Towns and Villages**: Cities like Annecy in France, Sintra in Portugal, and Ghent in Belgium offer stunning scenery, historical architecture, and a chance to see local life without large crowds.
- **Discover Hidden Neighborhoods**: Even major cities have pockets of culture and charm that many tourists miss. Explore places like Trastevere in Rome, Alfama in Lisbon, and El Raval in Barcelona for an authentic glimpse into the

daily life and spirit of the city.

- **Ask Locals for Recommendations**: Locals can guide you to hidden treasures. Ask for recommendations on places to eat, hidden viewpoints, and favorite local spots—they may lead you to places you'd never find in a guidebook.

Participating in Local Customs and Festivals

Europe is known for its festivals, seasonal markets, and unique traditions. Participating in these events gives you an insider's look into the culture:

- **Traditional Festivals**: Try to align your visit with local festivals like Oktoberfest in Munich, the Edinburgh Festival Fringe, or the annual Carnival in Venice for an unforgettable cultural experience.
- **Cultural Classes and Workshops**: Look for opportunities to join cooking classes in Italy, wine tasting in France, or flamenco lessons in Spain. These hands-on experiences offer a memorable way to connect with local culture.
- **Markets and Artisan Fairs**: Europe's markets, from Berlin's flea markets to London's Borough Market, are vibrant places to experience local food, art, and crafts. Don't miss seasonal events like the Christmas markets in Germany or the flower markets in the Netherlands.

5.2 Connecting with Locals and Other Travelers

One of the best parts of solo travel is the opportunity to meet people from different backgrounds, both locals and fellow travelers. Here's how to foster meaningful connections along the way.

Making Friends on the Road

Solo travel doesn't have to mean isolation; there are many ways to meet people who can enrich your experience:

- **Stay in Social Accommodations**: Hostels, guesthouses, and even some boutique hotels have social events where solo travelers can mingle. Many hostels offer group activities like city tours, pub crawls, and cooking nights.
- **Join Group Tours**: Local tours for small groups, such as bike tours, walking tours, or food tours, provide a comfortable way to meet others while experiencing the city.
- **Use Social Apps for Travelers**: Apps like Meetup, Couchsurfing, and even Instagram can connect you with people in the area. Some cities also have local WhatsApp or Facebook groups for travelers.

Engaging in Meaningful Conversations with Locals

Engaging with locals can deepen your understanding of a place and create lasting memories:

- **Learn Basic Phrases in the Local Language**: A few phrases like "hello," "thank you," and "goodbye" in the local language can make a positive impression and often lead to warm conversations.
- **Visit Local Cafés and Bookshops**: Cafés, bookshops, and local hangouts are great places to strike up casual conversations with locals.
- **Attend Language Exchange Meetups**: Many cities have language exchange events where people meet to practice different languages. It's a fun, relaxed way to meet locals and

improve language skills.

5.3 Capturing and Preserving Memories

Travel memories are precious, and finding ways to capture them can help you cherish your experiences long after you've returned home. Here's how to preserve those special moments creatively.

Taking Meaningful Photos

Rather than focusing only on capturing landmarks, try to document moments that capture the spirit of your journey:

- **Capture Everyday Moments**: Snap photos of local markets, meals, and street scenes that highlight the daily life of the place you're visiting.

- **Create a Photo Journal**: Keep a small notebook where you jot down details about each photo—where you were, what you felt, and any conversations you had. This turns your photos into a storytelling experience.
- **Use Self-Timers or Ask Others**: Don't hesitate to ask fellow travelers or locals to take your picture, or use a self-timer for solo shots. These photos capture you in the midst of your adventure and make great memories.

Keeping a Travel Journal

Journaling can be a reflective and enjoyable way to document your journey:

- **Write a Daily Recap**: Summarize your day in a few sentences—what you did, saw, and felt. This will create a memory bank you can revisit anytime.
- **Record Small Details**: Capture snippets of conversations, funny encounters, or meaningful moments in your journal. These little details are often what we forget over time.
- **Sketch Your Surroundings**: If you're artistically inclined, consider sketching some of the places you visit. Even simple sketches can be a meaningful way to remember special places.

5.4 Practicing Mindfulness and Gratitude

Solo travel can be deeply transformative, especially when you approach it mindfully. Slowing down and appreciating each experience allows you to make the most of your journey.

Embrace the Present Moment

Taking time to be mindful during your travels helps you savor each experience. Here's how to stay grounded on your journey:

- **Pause and Observe**: Instead of rushing through your itinerary, take a few moments at each destination to breathe, observe, and appreciate the setting.
- **Disconnect from Technology**: While documenting your trip is important, set aside some moments without your phone or camera. Embrace these times to absorb the beauty and atmosphere around you fully.
- **Reflect on Your Journey**: At the end of each day, take a few minutes to reflect on what you experienced and what you're grateful for. This can deepen your appreciation for the journey and help you internalize the memories.

Practicing Gratitude for the Journey

Traveling solo can be challenging, but it's also a privilege. Cultivating gratitude can enrich your experience:

- **Recognize Small Acts of Kindness**: Whether it's a friendly smile from a stranger, a helpful direction from a local, or a warm meal after a long day, take note of the kindness you encounter.
- **Celebrate Your Independence**: Each decision you make on your own is a testament to your strength and courage. Celebrate your ability to travel solo and the unique perspective it gives you on the world.
- **Be Grateful for the Opportunity to Explore**: Recognizing the privilege of travel, the places you see, and the cultures you

engage with will make your journey all the more meaningful.

5.5 Embracing the Journey as a Solo Traveler

Ultimately, solo travel is about self-discovery, growth, and pushing past comfort zones. Here's how to fully embrace this transformative journey.

Celebrate Your Solo Successes

Solo travel involves countless small victories, from navigating a new city alone to successfully communicating in a foreign language. Celebrate each achievement:

- **Reward Yourself with Small Treats**: Treat yourself to a favorite pastry, a souvenir, or a relaxing spa day. These small rewards can be a reminder of your accomplishments.
- **Reflect on Your Growth**: Solo travel often leads to personal growth. Take time to reflect on what you've learned about yourself, your preferences, and your boundaries.
- **Appreciate Your Resilience**: Traveling alone requires resilience, adaptability, and confidence. Embrace the strength and independence that you develop along the way.

Trust the Journey

Not every day will be perfect, but trust that each moment contributes to a meaningful experience:

- **Embrace the Unexpected**: Whether it's a delay in plans, a sudden change in weather, or an unplanned detour, embrace the unexpected moments. These often lead to the most memorable experiences.

- **Let Go of Perfection**: It's natural to want everything to go smoothly, but solo travel can be unpredictable. Letting go of perfection allows you to enjoy the journey fully.
- **Savor the Freedom of Solo Exploration**: There's a unique joy in exploring the world on your terms. Embrace the freedom to set your own pace, pursue your interests, and discover new passions.

5.6 Bringing the Journey Home

While the adventure may end, the impact of solo travel can last a lifetime. Here's how to keep the travel spirit alive after you've returned home.

Staying Connected with People You Met

If you made meaningful connections with fellow travelers or locals, stay in touch:

- **Exchange Social Media or Email**: Share contact information with people you connected with on the road. This allows you to maintain friendships or even plan future travels together.
- **Send a Thank-You Note**: If a local went out of their way to help or guide you, a small note or message of gratitude can mean a lot.

Reflecting on Your Experience

When you return, take time to look back on your journey:

- **Create a Travel Scrapbook**: Print photos, keep tickets, and collect little mementos to create a scrapbook of your travels.
- **Share Stories with Loved Ones**: Sharing your experiences with family and friends helps keep the memories alive and allows you to reflect on what you've learned.

Solo travel is a journey not only through new places but also within yourself. By seeking authentic experiences, connecting with locals, capturing meaningful memories, and embracing the journey with gratitude, you're creating stories and lessons that will stay with you long after you've returned. Europe awaits—let it be the backdrop for your own unforgettable solo adventure!

Chapter 6: Budgeting and Managing Finances for a Solo Adventure

Traveling through Europe as a solo adventurer can be done on almost any budget, as long as you plan strategically and make mindful spending decisions along the way. In this chapter, we'll discuss how to create a realistic budget, maximize savings before departure, and manage your expenses throughout your trip so you can enjoy every experience without financial stress.

6.1 Planning Your Budget and Setting Financial Goals

Before you start exploring Europe, it's essential to have a budget that covers all aspects of your journey, from flights to meals and souvenirs. Knowing how much you'll need for each category will help you avoid unexpected expenses.

Estimating Costs for Your Destination

The costs of travel vary greatly depending on the country and region within Europe. Here's how to estimate expenses for each part of your trip:

- **Accommodation**: Research the cost of hotels, hostels, and short-term rentals in your chosen destinations. Cities like London and Paris tend to be more expensive than smaller cities like Porto or Kraków.
- **Food and Dining**: Estimate daily meal costs by checking local restaurant prices. Also, consider whether you'll prepare some meals yourself to save money.
- **Transportation**: Consider flights, train passes, and public transportation. If you'll be traveling between multiple cities

or countries, look into rail passes like the Eurail or budget airlines like Ryanair.

- **Activities and Excursions**: Make a list of key activities you want to do, such as museum visits, guided tours, or outdoor excursions, and budget for entry fees or equipment rentals.

Creating a Travel Fund

Once you have an estimate, determine how much you need to save in advance:

- **Set Up a Dedicated Savings Account**: Open a savings account specifically for your travel fund. This keeps your travel savings separate from other funds, making it easier to track.
- **Automate Savings**: Set up an automatic transfer each month into your travel account. Even small amounts add up over time.
- **Cut Back on Daily Expenses**: Consider small sacrifices, like skipping the daily coffee shop run or reducing online subscriptions, to add more to your travel savings.

6.2 Saving Money on Transportation

Transportation can be a major expense, but with the right approach, you can save significantly on flights, trains, buses, and local transportation.

Booking Affordable Flights

If flying is necessary, booking smartly can save a lot:

- **Use Price-Comparison Sites**: Websites like Skyscanner and Google Flights help you find the best prices across airlines. Be flexible with dates to discover the cheapest options.
- **Consider Budget Airlines**: Europe has several budget carriers (like EasyJet and Ryanair) that offer affordable flights

between major cities. Just keep in mind that these airlines may charge for extra luggage or seat selection.

- **Opt for Red-Eye or Midweek Flights**: Traveling during off-peak times, such as weekdays or late-night flights, can lead to lower fares.

Maximizing Savings on Local and Regional Transportation

Traveling within Europe by bus or train is often cost-effective:

- **Rail Passes**: If you plan on visiting several countries, a Eurail or Interrail pass can be a great deal. These passes offer flexibility and allow you to hop on and off trains across Europe.
- **Bus Travel**: For budget-conscious travelers, buses like FlixBus and BlaBlaCar are inexpensive ways to move between cities, especially for shorter distances.
- **Public Transportation**: Use local buses, metros, and trams to get around cities. Many cities offer day passes or multi-day tickets at a discounted rate.

6.3 Finding Affordable Accommodation

Accommodation is another significant expense, but there are options to suit any budget, from hostels to vacation rentals.

Choosing Budget-Friendly Options

There are several types of affordable accommodations in Europe:

- **Hostels**: These are ideal for solo travelers, offering both dormitory and private rooms. Many hostels have communal kitchens, social activities, and tours that allow you to save money while meeting fellow travelers.

- **Guesthouses and B&Bs**: These small, family-owned establishments are often more affordable than hotels and provide a local experience.
- **Short-Term Rentals**: Platforms like Airbnb or Booking.com can offer unique stays at competitive prices, especially if you're staying for a few days or longer.

Using Points and Membership Discounts

If you frequently travel, join loyalty programs or use credit card points for savings:

- **Hotel Loyalty Programs**: Major hotel chains offer points for each stay that can lead to discounts or free nights.
- **Credit Card Points**: If you have a travel credit card, use points or rewards for flights, hotels, or rental cars.
- **Student, Senior, or Membership Discounts**: Certain hostels, tours, and transport services offer discounts for students, seniors, or members of organizations like Hostelling International or AAA.

6.4 Managing Daily Expenses on a Budget

Once on the road, keeping your daily expenses in check is essential to staying within budget. Here are some tips to manage spending without sacrificing experiences.

Eating Affordably Without Missing Out

Food is a highlight of European travel, and you can enjoy local flavors without breaking the bank:

- **Eat Like a Local**: Instead of dining at restaurants in tourist-heavy areas, explore local neighborhoods where prices are often lower, and food is authentic.
- **Visit Markets and Grocery Stores**: Local markets and grocery stores offer fresh produce, cheeses, and bread that you can use to make your own meals. Many markets also offer affordable ready-made meals.
- **Enjoy Lunch Specials**: Many restaurants in Europe offer discounted lunch menus, where you can get a full meal for less than you'd pay at dinnertime.

Tracking Expenses on the Go

Tracking your spending daily helps you stay within budget:

- **Use Budgeting Apps**: Apps like Trail Wallet, TravelSpend, or even a simple note on your phone can help you monitor expenses.
- **Set a Daily Spending Limit**: Divide your total budget by the number of days you'll be traveling to create a daily spending cap, leaving some extra for unexpected splurges.
- **Pay with Local Currency**: When using a credit card, always choose to pay in the local currency to avoid unfavorable exchange rates.

6.5 Dealing with Currency Exchange and Bank Fees

Managing foreign currency and understanding banking fees is essential for any international traveler. Here's how to handle money matters efficiently.

Using the Right Payment Methods

Using credit and debit cards abroad is generally safe and convenient, but it's important to plan for fees:

- **Get a Travel-Friendly Bank Account**: Many banks offer accounts that waive foreign transaction fees, making them ideal for international travel.
- **Use Local ATMs for Cash**: If you need cash, avoid currency

exchange kiosks in airports or tourist areas, as they often have high fees. Withdraw from a local ATM for better rates.

- **Carry a Backup Card**: Always have a second card or form of payment in case of loss, theft, or ATM issues.

Protecting Yourself from Fraud

When using credit cards and ATMs, be vigilant to avoid fraud:

- **Notify Your Bank**: Inform your bank of your travel plans to avoid having your card blocked due to suspicious activity.
- **Use ATMs in Secure Locations**: Opt for ATMs in banks or well-lit, populated areas to reduce the risk of card skimming.
- **Check Card Charges**: Regularly review your transactions to catch any suspicious charges early.

6.6 Budgeting for the Unexpected

Travel can come with surprises, and setting aside an emergency fund ensures you're prepared for anything from missed flights to spontaneous excursions.

Building a Travel Contingency Fund

An emergency fund gives you peace of mind for unexpected expenses:

- **Set Aside Extra Cash**: Reserve a portion of your budget specifically for unexpected costs, such as additional transportation, extra nights in accommodation, or unforeseen activities.
- **Use a Travel Insurance Plan**: Travel insurance can save you from substantial expenses if you encounter medical emergencies, trip cancellations, or lost luggage.

Preparing for Additional Costs

Beyond emergencies, factor in these often-overlooked expenses:

- **Tipping**: Tipping customs vary across Europe. In many countries, a small tip is appreciated but not required, while in others, like Spain, service is included.
- **Souvenirs and Shopping**: Plan ahead for keepsakes or gifts. Decide on a small shopping budget to avoid overspending on spur-of-the-moment buys.
- **Departure Taxes and Fees**: Some airports and cities require a departure tax. Research these fees ahead of time to include them in your budget.

Traveling solo on a budget in Europe is entirely possible with the right planning and a bit of flexibility. With your finances in order, you'll be free to enjoy the experiences that matter most—whether it's savoring a delicious meal, exploring an ancient site, or finding that perfect memento to remind you of your adventure. By budgeting thoughtfully and spending wisely, you can explore Europe confidently, with the financial freedom to make the most of every moment.

Chapter 7: Embracing the Journey: Joys and Challenges of Solo Travel

Solo travel is an incredible journey of independence, personal growth, and adventure. It offers an unmatched sense of freedom but also presents challenges that can test your resilience. This chapter will explore some common hurdles of traveling alone and practical strategies for overcoming them. Embracing both the highs and lows of solo travel can help you grow, discover new strengths, and leave you with memories that last a lifetime.

7.1 Facing Loneliness and Finding Fulfillment

One of the most common challenges of solo travel is feeling lonely at times, especially in unfamiliar surroundings. But solo travel can also provide the perfect setting for self-reflection, self-discovery, and personal fulfillment.

Navigating Moments of Loneliness

Traveling alone means you may occasionally miss familiar faces or yearn for companionship. Here are ways to cope with those moments:

- **Stay Connected with Loved Ones**: Keep in touch with

family and friends via messaging, video calls, or even postcards. Sharing parts of your journey can lessen feelings of isolation.

- **Journal Your Thoughts**: Writing about your experiences, thoughts, and emotions can be an excellent outlet. Journaling not only helps you process your feelings but also creates a record of your journey that you can look back on.
- **Embrace the Opportunity for Solitude**: Instead of avoiding alone time, learn to appreciate it. Solo travel provides a unique opportunity for self-reflection and helps you become comfortable with your own company.

Finding Fulfillment in the Experience

Solo travel offers numerous ways to cultivate a deep sense of fulfillment and purpose:

- **Set Personal Goals for the Trip**: Whether it's learning a few phrases in a new language, trying a particular dish, or pushing yourself to explore a challenging destination, set goals to focus on personal growth and celebrate achievements along the way.
- **Volunteer or Participate in Local Initiatives**: Many travelers find fulfillment through volunteer work, such as helping at a local animal shelter or joining a beach cleanup. Engaging in local initiatives helps you give back to the places you visit and connect with local people on a meaningful level.
- **Practice Gratitude Daily**: Spend a few minutes each day reflecting on what you're grateful for. Appreciating the privilege of travel and the beautiful experiences along the way can enhance your solo journey.

7.2 Managing Cultural Differences and Language Barriers

Traveling solo in a foreign country often means adapting to new customs and overcoming language barriers. Learning to navigate these challenges builds confidence and enriches your experience.

Handling Language Barriers

Learning even a few words or phrases in the local language can make a world of difference:

- **Learn Key Phrases Before You Go**: Basic phrases like "hello," "thank you," and "help, please" can go a long way in building rapport with locals. Use language apps like Duolingo or Babbel to practice before your trip.
- **Use Translation Apps**: Apps like Google Translate make it easy to communicate. Many translation apps also allow you to download languages for offline use, which can be a lifesaver in remote areas.
- **Rely on Nonverbal Communication**: Simple gestures, facial expressions, and body language can help bridge language gaps. Smiling, pointing, and showing polite gestures demonstrate friendliness and can break down language barriers.

Adapting to Cultural Differences

Different cultures have unique customs and expectations, and adapting to these differences shows respect and helps you feel more at ease:

- **Research Local Etiquette**: Familiarize yourself with local customs, especially regarding dress, table manners, and greetings. For example, in some parts of Europe, it's customary to greet with a kiss on both cheeks, while in others, a handshake is preferred.

- **Observe and Adapt**: Watch how locals behave in different settings—whether it's at a café, on public transport, or at a historical site. Observing and mimicking local behavior helps you blend in and show respect for the culture.
- **Be Open-Minded and Nonjudgmental**: Embrace cultural differences with curiosity rather than judgment. Solo travel allows you to learn about new ways of life, and approaching these differences with respect makes the experience more rewarding.

7.3 Staying Motivated and Positive on Long Journeys

Long trips or extended stays in foreign countries can sometimes lead to burnout or travel fatigue. Knowing how to stay motivated and find balance is key to making the most of your journey.

Balancing Exploration and Rest

Constant movement can be exhausting, even for the most enthusiastic travelers. Balance is essential to stay energized:

- **Take Rest Days**: Schedule "rest days" where you relax, catch up on sleep, or simply enjoy a leisurely day without an agenda. Use this time to recharge so you're ready for more exploration.
- **Create a Flexible Itinerary**: While it's tempting to see as much as possible, build flexibility into your itinerary. Allow time to wander, relax, or change plans without feeling rushed.
- **Practice Mindfulness**: Whether it's meditation, deep breathing, or simply pausing to appreciate a moment,

mindfulness practices help you stay present and positive during your journey.

Rediscovering Excitement When Motivation Wanes

Travel fatigue or homesickness can sometimes dampen your enthusiasm. Here's how to revive the excitement:

- **Rediscover Your 'Why'**: Remind yourself why you wanted to travel in the first place. Reflect on the personal goals or dreams that led you to embark on this adventure.
- **Switch Up Your Routine**: If you've been visiting museums and landmarks, try something different—take a cooking class, go hiking, or spend a day by the sea. Changing your activities can help refresh your perspective.
- **Connect with New People**: Meeting other travelers or locals often brings new energy and fresh insights. A friendly conversation, a shared meal, or an impromptu adventure can reignite your passion for travel.

7.4 Embracing Uncertainty and Adapting to Challenges

Solo travel is filled with surprises—some delightful and others challenging. Learning to embrace the unknown and adapt to unexpected situations is a valuable skill that extends beyond travel.

Expecting the Unexpected

Flexibility is crucial when you're on your own:

- **Let Go of Perfection**: Things may not always go according to plan. Weather, transportation delays, or changes in accommodation may require flexibility. Embracing imperfections helps reduce stress.

- **Embrace Serendipitous Moments**: Some of the most memorable travel experiences happen unexpectedly. Whether it's stumbling upon a hidden café, meeting a new friend, or discovering a festival, these surprises often create the best memories.
- **Be Open to Changing Plans**: Solo travel gives you the freedom to adapt plans without needing to accommodate anyone else. If a new opportunity arises, consider saying "yes" and seeing where it leads.

Learning from Challenges

Facing challenges alone can be empowering:

- **View Obstacles as Learning Opportunities**: Travel can come with hurdles, such as missed connections, language mix-ups, or cultural misunderstandings. Approach these obstacles as opportunities to grow and build resilience.
- **Celebrate Problem-Solving Skills**: Solo travel requires quick thinking and adaptability, which can boost your self-confidence. Each challenge you overcome reinforces your ability to handle future difficulties.
- **Reflect on Your Strengths**: Take a moment to appreciate the courage it takes to travel solo. Recognizing your strengths and capabilities can be empowering and help you face future challenges confidently.

7.5 The Joy of Self-Discovery and Personal Growth

Solo travel is a journey of self-discovery. Embracing the freedom, independence, and growth that come with traveling alone can be one of the most fulfilling aspects of the experience.

Finding Confidence in Independence

Traveling solo teaches you to rely on yourself and trust your abilities:

- **Celebrate Your Independence**: Each decision you make, from choosing your next destination to navigating a new city, reinforces your independence. Savor the freedom of doing things your way.
- **Trust Your Instincts**: Solo travel is a great opportunity to listen to your inner voice and trust your instincts. Whether it's choosing a restaurant, exploring a side street, or moving to a new city, trust yourself to make decisions that feel right for you.
- **Appreciate the Freedom to Explore**: Solo travel allows you

to set your own pace, follow your interests, and discover new passions. Enjoy the luxury of exploring without compromise.

Embracing the Lessons of Solo Travel

Solo travel isn't just about the places you see but also about the person you become along the way:

- **Reflect on Your Journey**: Take time to reflect on how travel has changed you. Journaling or sharing stories with loved ones helps you appreciate the growth you've experienced.
- **Take the Lessons Home**: The resilience, flexibility, and independence you develop on the road can benefit you long after the journey ends. Apply these lessons to your daily life, knowing that you've grown through each experience.
- **Cherish Your Achievements**: Solo travel takes courage, from stepping out of your comfort zone to navigating unfamiliar places. Celebrate each moment, each achievement, and each lesson learned along the way.

7.6 Continuing the Adventure After the Journey Ends

When your journey comes to an end, the memories and personal growth you've gained continue. Here's how to keep the spirit of solo travel alive once you're home.

Staying Connected with New Friends

If you made connections while traveling, stay in touch:

- **Keep in Contact**: Send messages, share photos, or even plan future trips with friends you made along the way. Many solo travelers find lifelong friends during their journeys.

- **Join Travel Communities**: Connect with online travel communities where you can share stories, find inspiration, and stay connected with like-minded adventurers.

Reflecting on Your Solo Journey

Returning home provides a chance to reflect on the impact of solo travel:

- **Document Your Experiences**: Consider creating a photo album, scrapbook, or travel blog to keep your memories alive.
- **Share Your Story**: Share your adventures and insights with friends or family. Your story may inspire others to set off on their own journeys.

Traveling solo is a path to self-discovery, resilience, and independence. Embrace every moment, savor every lesson, and know that the experiences you've had will stay with you for a lifetime. Europe is waiting, and with this guide, you're well-prepared to make your journey unforgettable. Enjoy every step of this grand adventure—your story is just beginning.

Chapter 8: Making Solo Travel a Lifelong Adventure

Congratulations! You've completed an incredible solo journey through Europe and gained countless new skills, experiences, and memories. But this adventure doesn't have to be the end. In fact, your first solo trip can mark the beginning of a lifelong passion for exploration. In this final chapter, we'll look at ways to sustain your love for solo travel, plan future adventures, and make traveling a continuous, enriching part of your life.

8.1 Reflecting on Your Journey and Discovering New

Goals

After any adventure, it's beneficial to take some time to look back, reflect on your experiences, and think about what you've learned. Reflecting not only helps you appreciate your journey but also gives you insight into what you want from future travel experiences.

Reflect on Personal Growth and Achievements

The challenges you faced and the rewards you enjoyed during solo travel have contributed to personal growth. Here's how to process and celebrate your journey:

- **Review Your Journal or Photos**: Go back through any journals, photos, or mementos from your trip. Reflect on each moment, from the small joys to the larger breakthroughs.
- **Write Down Lessons Learned**: Note any lessons, new skills, or surprising realizations you gained. Did solo travel make you more confident, adaptable, or resilient?
- **Celebrate Your Independence**: Solo travel is a big achievement! Take time to recognize and celebrate the independence and courage you demonstrated.

Set New Travel Goals

Now that you've completed one trip, think about what's next:

- **Explore a New Destination**: Perhaps there's another region or continent you've always wanted to explore. Use your first trip as a foundation for venturing farther.
- **Challenge Yourself with a Unique Experience**: Consider adding a twist to future trips, like hiking through national

parks, embarking on a wellness retreat, or taking a creative workshop in a foreign city.

- **Plan a Long-Term Travel Goal**: If solo travel has become a passion, start planning for longer adventures or consider a goal like visiting all European capitals or exploring each continent.

8.2 Maintaining the Travel Mindset at Home

The lessons, habits, and perspectives gained during solo travel don't have to end when you're back home. Embracing the travel mindset in everyday life keeps the adventure alive and enriches your daily experiences.

Stay Curious and Adventurous in Daily Life

Just as you explored unknown places and tried new things abroad, you can keep this spirit alive at home:

- **Explore Your Local Area**: Look for places in your own city or region that you haven't yet visited, such as museums, trails, or hidden gems. Exploring with a traveler's mindset can bring a sense of adventure to familiar surroundings.
- **Try New Hobbies or Interests**: Embrace the idea of learning something new, just like you did abroad. Try a cooking class, learn a language, or take up an outdoor activity you enjoyed while traveling.
- **Be Open to Meeting New People**: Solo travel helps you connect with people from diverse backgrounds. Continue this openness by attending local events or joining groups where you can meet others who share your interests.

Continue Practicing Gratitude and Mindfulness

Gratitude and mindfulness can help you appreciate the small joys in daily life:

- **Keep a Gratitude Journal**: Reflect on things you're grateful for each day, much like you did while traveling. This practice can help you find joy in ordinary moments and stay grounded.
- **Embrace Mindfulness**: Practice being present and enjoying each moment, just as you did while immersing yourself in new surroundings. Mindfulness helps you maintain a sense of peace and wonder in everyday life.

8.3 Expanding Your Solo Travel Network

Solo travel is an independent journey, but it doesn't mean you're alone in your experiences. Many solo travelers around the world share a similar passion, and connecting with them can inspire you and expand your perspective.

Join Solo Travel Communities

Connecting with other solo travelers is a great way to share stories, get advice, and find inspiration:

- **Online Travel Communities**: Platforms like Reddit, Solo

Traveler World, and various Facebook groups offer forums where solo travelers share experiences, tips, and encouragement.

- **Meetup Groups**: Look for local Meetup groups for solo travelers, adventurers, or those who enjoy exploring. These groups often host events, day trips, or even international adventures.
- **Attend Travel Events or Conferences**: Many cities host travel shows or conferences where you can meet fellow travelers, listen to inspiring speakers, and learn about new destinations.

Stay Connected with Friends You Made Abroad

The people you meet while traveling often share your adventurous spirit:

- **Keep in Touch Online**: Whether through social media, email, or messaging apps, stay connected with the friends you made on the road. Exchanging travel stories or planning future meetups keeps the bond alive.
- **Organize a Reunion Trip**: If you connected with other travelers during your trip, consider organizing a reunion in a new city or country. Meeting again for a shared adventure is a fantastic way to rekindle friendships.

8.4 Preparing for Your Next Solo Journey

Your first solo trip has given you valuable skills and insights that make planning your next adventure easier. Here are some tips to streamline the process and create an even better experience for future travels.

Refine Your Packing and Planning Routine

Each trip teaches us new packing and preparation tricks. Here's how to make packing and planning more efficient:

- **Create a Master Packing List**: Based on your last trip, create a list of essentials, things you missed, and items you could have done without. This list can serve as a template for future travels.
- **Streamline Planning with Travel Apps**: Use apps like Google Trips, Rome2Rio, or TripIt to organize your itinerary and travel information. Having everything in one place makes planning more manageable.
- **Try New Travel Gear**: If there's equipment or gear you wish you'd had (like a better travel bag or a compact water filter), consider investing in it for your next adventure.

Experiment with Different Travel Styles

Your first trip may have given you an idea of the travel styles you enjoy most, but it's worth exploring other options:

- **Consider Slow Travel**: Instead of moving from city to city, try staying in one place for a longer period to immerse yourself deeply in the local culture.
- **Try Different Accommodations**: If you stayed in hostels, perhaps try vacation rentals or guesthouses. Experimenting with various accommodations allows you to find the best fit for your travel preferences.
- **Venture into New Regions**: If you explored Europe, why not try Asia, South America, or Africa? Each region offers unique cultures, landscapes, and experiences that can add new

dimensions to your travel perspective.

8.5 Making Solo Travel Sustainable and Purposeful

As you expand your travels, consider how to make your adventures not only enjoyable but also responsible. Traveling sustainably and with purpose enhances both your experience and the world around you.

Practice Responsible Tourism

Traveling responsibly means being mindful of your impact on the environment and local communities:

- **Support Local Businesses**: Shop at local markets, eat at family-owned restaurants, and book tours with local guides.

This helps you support local economies and experience authentic culture.

- **Minimize Waste and Conserve Resources**: Carry a reusable water bottle, refuse plastic bags, and be mindful of energy usage. Small changes can make a significant difference in reducing your environmental impact.
- **Respect Local Customs and Traditions**: Being culturally sensitive helps preserve the authenticity of the places you visit. Familiarize yourself with local customs, dress appropriately, and always ask permission before taking photos of people or private spaces.

Consider Volunteering or Meaningful Travel

Some solo travelers find purpose by volunteering or engaging in projects that give back to the communities they visit:

- **Volunteer Opportunities**: Platforms like Workaway, WWOOF, and GoAbroad connect travelers with local communities and projects around the world, from teaching English to environmental conservation.
- **Participate in Cultural Exchange Programs**: Programs like language exchanges, homestays, or farm stays provide immersive experiences where you contribute to a community while gaining a deeper understanding of the culture.
- **Document Your Journey with Purpose**: Sharing your travel experiences through a blog, vlog, or social media can inspire others and create a platform for responsible travel advocacy.

8.6 Inspiring Others to Embark on Their Own Journey

One of the most fulfilling ways to continue your journey is to share it with others. Your solo travel experience has given you insights, confidence, and stories that can inspire friends, family, and even strangers to step out of their comfort zones.

Share Your Story

Inspire others by sharing your journey in a way that feels authentic to you:

- **Blog or Social Media**: Documenting your travels online allows you to share valuable insights, tips, and stories that may inspire others to travel solo.
- **Create a Travel Guide**: You could compile a list of your favorite places, activities, or tips from your experience to help others planning a similar journey.
- **Offer Advice to Aspiring Travelers**: Share advice with friends, family, or online communities. Let them know the benefits of solo travel and how they can overcome their own fears or uncertainties.

Encourage Friends to Try Solo Travel

Solo travel isn't for everyone, but some people may just need a little encouragement to try it:

- **Plan a Group Trip with Solo Days**: If friends are hesitant to travel solo, plan a trip where everyone spends a day or two exploring individually. This gives a taste of solo travel while still having the group for support.
- **Be a Mentor**: Offer to help someone with their solo travel planning, from finding flights to booking accommodations. Providing guidance can make solo travel feel more accessible.

Traveling solo has likely changed you in ways that will continue to unfold over time. As you head into the future, remember that each journey is unique, and there's no "right" way to travel. Follow your curiosity, honor your sense of adventure, and keep exploring—whether that means venturing to a new continent or finding beauty in your own backyard. Your solo travel journey is only beginning, and the world is filled with endless possibilities. So pack your bags, set new goals, and remember: the adventure of a lifetime is waiting for you, one solo journey at a time. Safe travels!

Chapter 9: Building a Lifestyle Around Solo Travel

Solo travel can be much more than a one-time adventure; for many, it becomes a lifelong passion woven into their everyday lives. Whether you aim to travel long-term, take short solo trips between work commitments, or incorporate the traveler's mindset into your routine, this chapter will guide you in balancing a love for solo travel with your career, relationships, and personal goals. Let's explore how to make travel a sustainable, fulfilling lifestyle choice.

9.1 Creating a Travel-Friendly Lifestyle

Living a life that supports regular travel, especially solo travel, requires a bit of planning and a flexible mindset. Here are some ways to design your life to accommodate more solo adventures, no matter your personal or professional commitments.

Set Intentional Travel Goals

Defining what you want from future travels can help you plan around your needs and lifestyle:

- **Plan Trips Around Milestones or Breaks**: Look for opportunities within your schedule, such as holidays, long weekends, or personal milestones (like birthdays or anniversaries). Planning around these dates makes travel more sustainable and memorable.
- **Create a Yearly Travel Plan**: Try to schedule one or two solo trips each year, keeping in mind how much time, budget, and flexibility you have.
- **Alternate Between Short and Long Trips**: If a month-long

adventure isn't feasible every year, opt for shorter getaways in between larger trips to keep the excitement alive.

Align Travel with Career Opportunities

Finding ways to travel through work can make frequent adventures more practical:

- **Look for Remote Work Options**: If your job allows, request remote days or even transition to fully remote work. This setup lets you travel to new places without taking extended time off.
- **Seek Out Travel-Based Roles**: Certain fields—such as consulting, teaching, or working for international organizations—offer frequent travel opportunities. These roles may allow you to see the world while progressing in your career.
- **Consider Freelancing or Short-Term Contracts**: If traditional employment restricts your travel, freelancing or short-term contracts may allow for greater freedom. Many freelancers balance work with travel by taking their projects on the road.

9.2 Building a Financial Plan for Frequent Travel

Frequent travel can add up, but with smart budgeting and financial planning, it's possible to make solo travel a regular part of life without breaking the bank. Here's how to manage your finances to support your travel dreams.

Budget for Travel Year-Round

Creating a dedicated travel fund can help you save consistently:

- **Automate Savings for Travel**: Set up a separate savings account for travel and automate monthly deposits. Even small amounts add up over time, giving you a steady fund for future adventures.
- **Prioritize Travel in Your Budget**: If solo travel is a high priority, re-evaluate other spending areas (like dining out or subscription services) and redirect those funds toward your travel budget.
- **Research Low-Cost Destinations**: Some regions, like Southeast Asia or parts of Eastern Europe, are particularly budget-friendly for solo travelers. Balancing high-cost and low-cost destinations makes frequent travel more affordable.

Earn and Use Travel Rewards

Loyalty programs and travel rewards make frequent travel much more affordable:

- **Use Travel Credit Cards**: Many travel credit cards offer rewards points, cash back, and discounts on airfare and hotels. Use these cards for everyday purchases to build up points for future travel.
- **Sign Up for Airline and Hotel Loyalty Programs**: Enroll in loyalty programs for airlines, hotels, and even rideshares. Points accumulate over time and can often be redeemed for free or discounted trips.
- **Hunt for Deals and Promotions**: Subscribe to travel deal websites and follow airlines and hotels on social media. This way, you're always aware of promotions and discounts to take advantage of.

9.3 Balancing Travel with Relationships and Family

Solo travel doesn't have to mean sacrificing relationships or missing out on quality time with loved ones. In fact, sharing stories and inviting others to join you occasionally can enhance your journey.

Involve Loved Ones in Your Travel Plans

Sharing your travel goals with family and friends helps them understand and support your lifestyle:

- **Communicate Your Travel Goals**: Let loved ones know why travel is important to you and what you gain from solo adventures. This opens up discussions about how you can keep in touch and support one another while you're away.

- **Plan Group Trips or Meet-Ups**: Invite friends or family to join you for part of a trip. Having a few shared experiences can help them feel connected to your adventures and see firsthand why travel is so meaningful to you.
- **Document and Share Your Journey**: Regularly sharing photos, stories, or blogs with family and friends keeps them involved in your journey. Staying connected helps maintain bonds even while you're away.

Stay Connected While Traveling

Maintaining close relationships while on the road is easier than ever with technology:

- **Schedule Calls and Video Chats**: Set aside time for regular check-ins with loved ones. Scheduling these in advance keeps relationships strong and helps family feel reassured.
- **Share Your Itinerary**: For safety and peace of mind, share your itinerary or a map of your travels with trusted family members.
- **Use Messaging Apps**: Apps like WhatsApp, Signal, and Messenger make it easy to send updates, photos, or even quick messages throughout your travels.

9.4 Embracing "Micro-Adventures" Between Big Trips

When extended travel isn't possible, you can keep the spirit of exploration alive through smaller adventures close to home. These "micro-adventures" bring the thrill of travel into your daily life.

Explore Local Hidden Gems

Your own area may hold untapped travel potential:

- **Research Local Attractions**: Visit a nearby town, nature reserve, or historical site you've never explored. Treat it as you would any travel destination—learn its history, explore its neighborhoods, and find hidden spots.
- **Engage in Local Festivals and Cultural Events**: Attend local food festivals, cultural fairs, or music events. These experiences can give you a taste of other cultures right at home.
- **Take Day Trips or Weekend Getaways**: If you live near natural attractions, beaches, or cities, plan quick getaways. A night or two away can bring the refreshment of travel without the need for extended time off.

Stay Curious in Your Daily Life

Apply the curiosity of travel to your everyday life by exploring new activities and routines:

- **Try New Hobbies or Activities**: Take a cooking class, try a new workout, or learn a skill. Solo travel is about self-discovery, and these activities can replicate that sense of newness at home.
- **Connect with People from Different Cultures**: Meet new people through international meet-ups, language exchanges, or cultural events. These connections can broaden your worldview and bring a sense of travel's diversity into your everyday routine.

9.5 Setting Long-Term Travel Goals

If you envision travel as a lifelong pursuit, having a few long-term goals can give your adventures a purpose. These goals add structure and make each trip feel like part of a larger journey.

Create a Travel "Bucket List"

Dreaming big and writing down your travel aspirations can motivate you to keep exploring:

- **Prioritize Meaningful Destinations**: List countries, cities, or specific landmarks you've always wanted to visit, whether it's trekking in Patagonia, seeing the Northern Lights, or exploring ancient ruins in Greece.

- **Add Thematic Goals**: Some travelers focus on unique themes, such as visiting all the national parks, seeing UNESCO World Heritage Sites, or exploring places known for specific cuisines or art.
- **Stay Open to Spontaneous Opportunities**: Keep your list open-ended to leave room for unexpected destinations or opportunities. Sometimes, the most memorable adventures are the unplanned ones.

Consider Travel-Based Personal Projects

Having a personal project tied to your travels can deepen your experience:

- **Photography or Videography Project**: Document your journeys through a specific lens, like photographing historical architecture or capturing street life.
- **Language Learning Goal**: Challenge yourself to learn the basics of a new language for each country you visit, or become fluent in a language over the course of multiple trips.
- **Volunteering or Giving Back**: You might plan annual trips to volunteer in meaningful projects, like conservation, education, or community building. Combining travel with giving back can add a profound sense of purpose to your adventures.

9.6 Living as a Lifelong Traveler

Whether you're at home or abroad, a travel mindset can bring you joy, resilience, and curiosity throughout your life. Solo travel isn't just about exploring new places; it's about expanding your horizons in every sense and living as an eternal explorer.

Cultivate the "Traveler's Mindset"

Applying the attitudes you developed during solo travel to everyday life can make even ordinary moments feel special:

- **Embrace Change and New Experiences**: Travel teaches you to adapt quickly, stay curious, and seek out the unknown. Use these lessons to approach challenges and new opportunities with an open mind.
- **Practice Flexibility and Patience**: Solo travel often requires flexibility and patience. Applying these skills to everyday situations helps you stay calm and adapt to life's inevitable surprises.
- **Seek Continuous Learning**: Just as travel helps you learn about new places and cultures, a traveler's mindset is one of lifelong learning. Read books, take classes, and stay curious about the world.

Inspire Others to Travel

Sharing your experiences and encouraging others to step out of their comfort zones can spread the joys of solo travel:

- **Be a Resource**: Offer tips, share itineraries, and encourage friends and family to try solo travel. You may inspire someone to take that first step toward an unforgettable journey.
- **Document Your Journeys**: Consider creating a blog, social media account, or even a book to share your solo travel experiences. Your stories can inspire and empower others to

explore the world.

- **Create a Community**: Organize events, meet-ups, or travel groups in your local area to connect with other travelers. Building a community of like-minded people can bring a sense of connection and belonging.

As you close this chapter, remember that travel is as much about the journey as it is about the destination. Making solo travel a continuous part of your life is about embracing growth, joy, and curiosity, wherever you are. May you keep exploring, discovering, and sharing your adventures with the world. Safe travels, fellow adventurer—your journey is just beginning!

This concludes the guide to embracing and incorporating solo travel as a lifestyle. Now, you have the tools and inspiration to keep the spirit of solo travel alive, no matter where life takes you. Enjoy the journey!

Don't miss out!

Visit the website below and you can sign up to receive emails whenever Derek McNeill publishes a new book. There's no charge and no obligation.

https://books2read.com/r/B-A-GSKQC-FYCEF

BOOKS 2 READ

Connecting independent readers to independent writers.

Also by Derek McNeill

Solar Energy Simplified. Unlock The Power Of The Sun With A Comprehensive Guide To Clean Solar Energy

Empowering Solo Women Travelers in Europe -The Ultimate Guide

Watch for more at deekstar.com.

About the Author

Derek McNeill is a seasoned traveler, explorer, and publisher with a passion for sharing the transformative power of solo adventures. With a lifetime of journeys across six continents, McNeill brings a wealth of firsthand knowledge about navigating new cultures and landscapes with confidence and curiosity. Beyond the thrill of discovery, McNeill is a committed advocate for sustainable energy, travel and a healthy green future. As a practicing 'conservationist', McNeill focuses on ways we as a responsible species can protect and honor the natural world.

Through writing, speaking, and mentorship, McNeill has inspired others to explore, mindfully, deeper connections to nature and encourages positive contributions to the world we live in, wherever we are. One example of the urge to write about his experiences was whilst touring the Greek islands in the early 80s.He saw Solar Power's future potential. He was amazed at how many Greek island homes were already 'Sun energy' self sufficient, a futuristic idea at that time. Decades later and after much research, McNeill, with much help and many resources, has compiled this comprehensive guide on the subject of Solar Power for the DIY Solar energy enthusiast.

Read more at deekstar.com.